The Glory of the
NATIVITY

The Glory of the NATIVITY

CLARE HAWORTH-MADEN
Editor

Saraband

Page 1: Madonna and Child with Saints John the Baptist and Sebastian, *by Pietro Perugino, 1493.*

Page 2: *A detail from* The Adoration of the Magi, *by Fra Angelico with Filippo Lippi, c. 1452–3.*

Page 3: *A detail from Giotto's* The Flight Into Egypt, *c. 1304–6.*

Published by Saraband (Scotland) Limited,
The Arthouse, 752–756 Argyle Street,
Glasgow G3 8UJ, Scotland
hermes@saraband.net

ISBN: 1-887354-37-9

Printed in China

10 9 8 7 6 5 4 3 2 1

Acknowledgements
Extracts from the Authorized Version of the Bible (The King James Bible), the rights in which are vested in the Crown, are reproduced by permission of the Crown's Patentee, Cambridge University Press.

The publisher would like to thank the following people for their assistance in the preparation of this book: Clare Haworth-Maden, Debbie Hayes, Sara Hunt, Phoebe Wong, Nicola Gillies, and Wendy J. Ciaccia Eurell. Grateful acknowledgement is also made for the illustrations featured in this book, which are reproduced by courtesy of Planet Art, 2002 Arttoday.com, Inc., and CorelDraw, except that of page 20, which is courtesy of Saraband Image Library.

This book is fondly dedicated to Robin Sommer.

Contents

INTRODUCTION

For unto us a child is born, unto us a son is given: and the governments shall be upon his shoulder: and his name shall be called Wonderful, Counsellor, The mighty God, The everlasting Father, The Prince of Peace.

Of the increase of his government and peace there shall be no end, upon the throne of David, and upon his kingdom, to order it, and to establish it with judgment and with justice from henceforth even for ever. The zeal of the LORD of hosts will perform this.

—ISAIAH 9:6–7

Right: Titian's Madonna and Child *is a touching evocation of the Virgin Mary's awe at finding herself the mother of the son of God, as well as of her tenderness for the divine infant.*

Every year on December 25, Christians celebrate the birth, or Nativity, of Jesus Christ, which occurred over two thousand years ago. No other birth has been depicted so frequently by artists over the centuries as that of the Christ child, while the carols that the Christian community sings during Advent, and the Nativity plays performed by children, have made even nonpracticing Christians familiar with the events surrounding Christ's birth.

Our knowledge of the Nativity stems from the New Testament gospels of St. Matthew and St. Luke, parts of which are reproduced in the pages that follow. Yet as we will see, underlying their accounts is a far more complex, and ancient, story than a straightforward reading of their words suggests.

The Gospels of St. Matthew and St. Luke

Of the four gospels of the New Testament, only those of St. Matthew and St. Luke tell of Christ's birth and the circumstances surrounding it. Scholars have suggested that Mark, who is believed to have been John Mark, an associate of Barnabas, Paul, and Peter, the first pope, was more concerned with cutting to the chase and describing the actions and work of Jesus, the man, in an attempt to draw Roman Gentiles to Christianity, while the intention of John, one of Christ's apostles, in writing his gospel was similarly to expand upon Jesus' teaching and message and thus to deepen the faith of existing believers.

Although the ultimate aim of Matthew and Luke's gospels was certainly also to inform, convince, and convert nonbelievers, as well as to strengthen the devotion of Christians, it seems that their purpose, as well as the audiences that they targeted, differed subtly from those of Mark and John.

Matthew is thought to have been Matthew Levi, another of Christ's apostles, who was primarily writing for fellow Jews, whether or not they had become Christians. Luke, on the other hand, is believed to have been a Syrian physician from Antioch—and thus a Gentile Christian—whose gospel was addressed to Theophilus, a Greek, "That thou mightest know the certainty of those things, wherein thou hast been instructed" (Luke 1:4), suggesting that Theophilus was either interested in becoming a Christian or a recent convert. It therefore seems that Luke's gospel was primarily aimed at a Gentile readership, and that Luke was furthermore concerned with presenting a factual story of Jesus' life as related by those "which from the beginning were eyewitnesses, and ministers of the word" (Luke 1:2), one of whom may have been the Virgin Mary herself.

Jesus, the Messiah

Reflecting the different preoccupations of Matthew and Luke's Jewish and Gentile readerships, the theme running through Matthew's gospel is that Jesus is the Jewish Messiah whose coming was prophesied in the Old Testament, while that of Luke is that Jesus is the savior of humankind, and not just of the "children of Israel," God's "chosen people."

Although both include Christ's line of descent in their gospels (Matthew 1:1–17 and Luke 3:23–38), and King David is common to both, the lists of Jesus' forebears not only differ, but while Matthew traces his ancestors back to Abraham (the father of the Hebrew people), Luke goes farther, to God, the creator of Adam, the first man, thereby emphasizing that Jesus was truly the "son of God" (and, indeed, Jesus often addresses God as "Father" in the gospels).

That Jesus counted King David, the founder of the royal Judean dynasty, among His ancestors has profound importance for Jews, who regard much of the period when David ruled over a united Israel as a golden age. On his death (which, historians speculate, occurred between 1018 and 970 BC), David proclaimed that God is "the tower of salvation for his king: and sheweth mercy to his anointed,

unto David, and to his seed for evermore" (2 Samuel 51). "Messiah," which is derived from the Hebrew *mashiah*, means "anointed one," as does "Christ," the anglicized version of the Greek *Christos*, the significance of being anointed lying in the Jewish practice of dedicating a person or object to a sacred purpose through anointment with oil, symbolizing the Holy Spirit.

At the time of Christ's Nativity, the once mighty nation of Israel was in ruins. Palestine, and thus Judea, was now part of Syria, a dominion of the Roman Emperor Augustus

Right: *The Old Testament prophet Jeremiah (depicted here by Michelangelo), who prophesied Christ's Nativity, ended his days in Egypt following the destruction of Jerusalem in 585 BC by the forces of the Babylonian King Nebuchadnezzar.*

Caesar (Octavian) that was governed by the pro-Roman Edomite King Herod the Great. This humiliating state of affairs intensified the Jewish people's longing for the coming of their Messiah, who, the Old Testament prophets had promised, would destroy Israel's enemies, restore the nation of Israel, and recreate the kingdom of God on Earth under his righteous, and peaceful, rule. They expected the Messiah to be a descendant of David, as foretold, for instance, by Jeremiah: "Behold, the days come, saith the LORD, that I will raise unto David a righteous Branch, and a King shall reign and prosper, and shall execute judgment and justice in the earth. In his days Judah shall be saved, and Israel shall dwell safely: and this is his name whereby he shall be called THE LORD OUR RIGHTEOUSNESS" (Jeremiah 23:5–6). And in Matthew 21:9, we are told that on Jesus' entry into Jerusalem, He was hailed as the "Son of David," thereby underlining the link between Jesus, David, and the Messiah. Matthew seems to further emphasize Jesus' status as the Davidic Messiah by specifying (in Matthew 1:17) that three sets of fourteen generations preceded Christ's birth, for in the Hebrew system of numerology, the Hebrew characters that make up David's name add up to fourteen. In addition, the eras covered by those generations represent the respective pre-eminence of the prophets, kings, and priests, the implication being that Jesus' birth had initiated a new generation, and consequently a new age.

It may seem strange that both Matthew and Luke state that Jesus was descended from David through Joseph, who, after all, was not actually His father. The explanation may be that they were asserting His legal right, as a child whose mother was married to Joseph, to claim David as His ancestor.

Above: *Solomon was the last king to rule over a united Israel. The son of King David and Bathsheba, "her that had been the wife of Urias [Uriah]" (Matthew 1:6), was renowned for his wisdom, his judgment in deciding which of two women fighting over a child was its mother being particularly celebrated.*

Time and time again the gospels draw a parallel between the events of Jesus' life and the Messiah described by the Old Testament prophets (see, for example, Isaiah 53 and Psalm 22, "a psalm of David"), a connection that Matthew frequently stresses with the words: "Now all this was done, that it might be fulfilled which was spoken of the Lord by the prophet" (Matthew 1:22). The name "Jesus," which, as a variant of Joshua, means "God saves" in Hebrew, is redolent of the Messiah, too, and Matthew tells us that an angel instructed Joseph to call Mary's unborn child "Jesus: for he shall save his people from their sins." Jesus asserted His status and mission in Luke 21:8 ("I am *Christ*") and Luke 24:46, when, after His resurrection, He confirmed to His disciples that He was indeed the Messiah of whose coming the prophets had told: "These *are* the words which I spake unto you, while I was yet with you, that all things must be fulfilled, which were written in the law of Moses, and *in* the prophets, and *in* the psalms, concerning me."

The identification of Jesus as the Messiah deepens our understanding of the story of the Nativity, as well as of the preordained events that led to His Passion and death. Christians believe that although Jesus was the Messiah, His work is not yet done. For Christ will return, and His second coming will be the day of judgment, when sinners are punished and the righteous will live in God's kingdom forever after. Armed with this knowledge, let us now look more closely at Matthew and Luke's accounts of the Nativity.

Opposite: Because John the Baptist saluted Jesus with the words "Behold the Lamb of God, which taketh away the sin of the world" (John 1:29) when they encountered one another as adults, he is often portrayed with a lamb, as in this Hieronymus Bosch painting.

THE CONCEPTION AND BIRTH OF JOHN THE BAPTIST

Luke begins his gospel by relating the miraculous circumstances surrounding the conception and birth of John the Baptist, thereby heralding the ministry of Jesus, as also asserted by Mark: "As it is written in the prophets, Behold, I send my messenger before thy face, which shall prepare thy

way before ye." (Mark 1:2). Luke identifies John with Elias (Luke 1:17), the Greek form of the name of the prophet Elijah, who, according to Malachi 4:5, God will send "before the great and dreadful day of the LORD." It has been said that John is the link between the Old Testament and the New, and Luke makes it clear through the words of the angel Gabriel, God's messenger, that his miraculous conception and birth to an elderly couple was predestined. By decreeing that the baby should be called John, which means "God has favored" in Hebrew, rather than Zacharias, after his father, as would have been customary, Gabriel emphasized the special qualities that would enable John to fulfill his role as a prophet in preparing the way for Christ.

As an adult, "John did baptize in the wilderness, and preach the baptism of repentance and the remission of sins" (Mark 1:4), his baptism of Jesus in the River Jordan causing the Holy Spirit to descend upon Jesus, God to recognize him as his son, and his work to begin.

THE CONCEPTION OF JESUS AND THE ANNUNCIATION

Matthew tells us that Mary became pregnant with Jesus before she had "come together" with Joseph, a carpenter of Nazareth to whom she was betrothed, and that Joseph was therefore considering rejecting her until an angel appeared to him in a dream explaining that the father of her child

was the Holy Ghost. In Matthew 1:23, the angel repeats almost
verbatim the words of the prophet Isaiah, "Therefore the
Lord himself shall give you a sign; Behold, a virgin shall
conceive, and bear a son, and shall call his name Immanuel"
(Isaiah 7:14), Matthew adding that "Emmanuel" means "God
with us" (meaning, "God is among us in the world of men"),
thereby convincing Joseph to stand by Mary and go through
with the marriage.

Luke, by contrast, relates that the angel Gabriel made the Annunciation (the announcement of the incarnation of the son of God in human form) to Mary, rather than Joseph, at the same time informing her that her cousin Elisabeth, the future mother of John the Baptist, was six months pregnant. Mary rushed to visit her cousin, whereupon Elisabeth felt her baby leap in her womb for joy and addressed the younger Mary as "the mother of my Lord." Thanks to His parentage, Mary's unborn child was both the son of God and the "son of Man" referred to in Daniel 7:13–14 as the Messiah.

Right: Luke (2:13–14) tells us that the shepherds witnessed "a multitude of the heavenly host praising God, and saying, Glory to God in the highest, and on earth peace, good will toward men" in celebration of Jesus' miraculous birth.

Left: *Correggio's interpretation of the Nativity is inspired by Luke's gospel, in which we are told that Mary laid her newborn son in a humble manger because there was no room for them in the inn (Luke 2:7).*

THE NATIVITY

Both Matthew and Luke give Jesus' place of birth as Bethlehem, Luke taking pains to explain why Mary and Joseph had left Nazareth, where they were living, to go there, namely to comply with the Roman emperor's decree that his subjects should be taxed in their birthplaces. As Joseph was the head of the family, he and his wife duly traveled to Bethlehem, which, as a descendent of David (once a lowly shepherd of Bethlehem), was his hometown. Crucially, the birth of Jesus in Bethlehem fulfilled a prophecy made in Micah 5:2: "But thou, Bethlehem Ephratah, *though* thou be little among the thousands of Judah, *yet* out of thee shall he come forth unto me *that is* to be ruler in Israel."

The gospels' accounts of the Nativity otherwise differ, with only Luke telling us that Jesus was laid in a manger, there being no room available in teeming Bethlehem, and that an angel called shepherds in the vicinity to witness Jesus' manifestation on earth and glorify him.

And it is only from Matthew that we learn of the adoration of Jesus by the wise men, who had been alerted to the birth of the "King of the Jews" by the presence of "his star in the

east." It is probable that the wise men, or Magi, were Chaldean Persian, or Arabian astrologers who were skilled in the art of interpreting heavenly signs, and who, perhaps being familiar with Jewish Messianic belief, concluded that the star that had newly appeared in the night sky signaled the birth of the Messiah. In this way, Matthew underlines the significance of Jesus' birth to non-Jews, as well as to men whose wisdom commanded respect. Medieval tradition felt it apt to upgrade the Magi to kings, each representing one of the three continents that were known at that time, namely Europe, Africa, and Asia, thereby emphasizing the humility that these powerful men felt in the presence of the infant Jesus. Matthew does not specify the number of wise men but the kings were later said to be three: Melchior, the giver of gold, Caspar, whose gift was frankincense, and Balthasar who brought myrrh. Matthew does, however, list these gifts no doubt on account of their symbolic and prophetic significance: gold denoting royalty; frankincense, or incense the worship of God; and myrrh being a substance that was used to prepare bodies for burial, so that together these gifts signifed Jesus' kingship, divinity, mortality, and death.

THE PRESENTATION IN THE TEMPLE

According to Mosaic law (Leviticus 12), after giving birth to a male child, a Jewish woman is unclean for seven days (and her son must be circumcised when eight days old). Thirty-three days later, she must bring a lamb and pigeon or turtledove, or if a lamb is out of the question, two pigeons or turtledoves, to the temple for a priest to sacrifice and atone for her sins, whereupon she is cleansed. Luke confirms that Mary and Joseph abided by Mosaic law, combining her purification ritual with Jesus' presentation in the temple (in Jerusalem), as was customary for baby boys. There, Jesus was recognized and saluted as the Messiah by both Simeon (a devout old man whom the Holy Ghost had told would see the "Lord's Christ" before he died, "A light to lighten the Gentiles, and the glory of thy people Israel") and the prophetess Anna. Luke makes it clear that this was no ordinary baby!

Below: Bellini's painting depicts the moment when Simeon took the Christ child into his arms in the temple "and blessed God and said, Lord, now lettest thou thy servant depart in peace, according to thy word: For mine eyes have seen thy salvation" (Luke 2:28–30).

THE HOLY FAMILY LEAVES BETHLEHEM

Opposite: A Greek icon portraying Jesus as a grown man on the verge of fulfilling His destiny, the redemption of humankind through His suffering and cruel death.

As they searched for the baby that was "born King of the Jews," Matthew says that the wise men approached King Herod, hoping that he would know the child's whereabouts, thereby alerting the paranoid king to the birth of a potential challenger to his power, his concern being deepened by the chief priests' assertion that the Messiah would be born in Bethlehem. Although he accordingly sent the wise men to Bethlehem, and tried to trick them into returning to inform him of Jesus' location, they were warned of his evil purposes in a dream, and set off for their homeland without seeing Herod again. Matthew tells us that the enraged Herod tried to eliminate the infant's threat to his kingship by ordering that all children under two years of age in Bethlehem and thereabouts should be slaughtered. When this terrible precautionary measure had been carried out, Matthew goes on to say that the voice of Rachel, a mother figure of Israel who died in childbirth in Ramah, on the way to Bethlehem, could be heard lamenting the massacre.

Right: According to Matthew, an angel appeared to Joseph three times in a dream: firstly, to inform him that Mary had conceived a child by the Holy Ghost; secondly, to warn him to take his family and flee into Egypt to save their son's life; and thirdly, to tell him that it was safe to return home to Israel.

Having been alerted to Herod's deadly intent by an angel in a dream, Joseph had managed to spirit Mary and Jesus away to Egypt (thus fulfilling a prophecy that the son of God would come from Egypt) before the massacre began. Here, according to Matthew, they remained until Herod was dead. On hearing that Herod's son, Achelaus, had assumed the rulership of Judea, Joseph deemed it unsafe to venture to Bethlehem, and so it was that the Holy Family settled in Nazareth, in Galilee. Although Matthew's story of the wise men, Herod, and the Flight into Egypt are absent from Luke's account of the Nativity, Luke also confirms that they returned to Nazareth following Jesus' birth.

Right: Unlike deciduous trees, evergreens never shed their leaves, even when covered in a blanket of winter snow, which is why the Christmas tree is a potent symbol of immortality and of the resurrected Christ.

CHRISTMAS

Throughout Advent (which starts on the first Sunday after November 30), Christians anticipate the anniversary of Christ's Nativity on December 25. It is a time when the words of the gospels ring out in the form of carols, Bible readings, and young actors' lines, even if these sometimes owe more to medieval additions and embellishments than to the New Testament. Christmastide traditionally ends on January 6, Twelfth Night, or the feast of the Epiphany (from the Greek *epiphaneia*, "an appearing"), which commemorates the manifestation of Christ to the Magi in the Western Church. Yet nowhere in the New Testament is it stated that the events of the Nativity occurred on these dates, so why are they celebrated then?

The answer has ancient roots that are grounded in Sun worship. The winter solstice, which can vary from year to year, but falls around December 22, heralds the weak winter Sun's increasing strength, which will reach its height at the summer solstice (around June 21). Pagan peoples consequently hailed the winter solstice as the occasion of the rebirth of the Sun god, whose decline, and eventual death, was believed to follow the autumnal equinox (on around September 23). The Romans, for example, saluted Sol Invictus, "the

Right: Giotto's beautiful portrayal of the First Christmas at Greccio, Italy, where St. Francis first recreated the Nativity scene (1223), beginning the traditional Christmas celebration that continues to this day.

unconquerable Sun," on December 25. Having found it impossible to eradicate the vestiges of such deep-rooted traditions, during the fourth century, the Christian Church simply imposed its own celebration, that of the Nativity, on its age-old predecessors. Similarly, the Christian Feast of the Annunciation, or Lady Day, which recalls the angel's appearance to Mary, falls on March 25, nine months before the supposed birth of Christ, but also around the date of the vernal equinox, one of the four great Sun festivals.

Right: *The Holy Family—Jesus, Mary, and Joseph—as depicted by Raphael. The lamb that the infant Jesus is embracing represents his role as a sacrificial lamb whose innocent blood will wash away humankind's sins.*

Jesus' Earthly Family

JESUS' FOREFATHERS

Previous page:
*Raphael envisaged
Mary and Joseph's
wedding ceremony as
taking place before a
magnificent temple.
Their marriage is
barely mentioned in
the gospels, however.*

1 The book of the generation of Jesus Christ, the son of David, the son of Abraham.

2 Abraham begat Isaac; and Isaac begat Jacob; and Jacob begat Judas and his brethren;

3 And Judas begat Phares and Zara of Thamar; and Phares begat Esrom; and Esrom begat Aram;

4 And Aram begat Aminadab; and Aminadab begat Naasson; and Naasson begat Salmon;

5 And Salmon begat Booz of Rachab; and Booz begat Obed of Ruth; and Obed begat Jesse;

6 And Jesse begat David the king; and David the king begat Solomon of her *that had been the wife of Urias;*

7 And Solomon begat Roboam; and Roboam begat Abia; and Abia begat Asa;

8 And Asa begat Josaphat; and Josaphat begat Joram; and Joram begat Ozias;

9 And Ozias begat Joatham; and Joatham begat Achaz; and Achaz begat Ezekias;

10 And Ezekias begat Manasses; and Manasses begat Amon; and Amon begat Josias;

11 And Josias begat Jechonias and his brethren, about the time they were carried away to Babylon:

12 And after they were brought to Babylon, Jechonias begat

Right: Michelangelo's lunettes of Jesus' ancestors, as listed by Matthew, in the Sistine Chapel include portrayals of Jacob, whose son, Joseph, married the Virgin Mary.

Salathiel; and Salathiel begat Zorobabel;

13 And Zorobabel begat Abiud; and Abiud begat Eliakim; and Eliakim begat Azor;

14 And Azor begat Sadoc; and Sadoc begat Achim; and Achim begat Eliud;

15 And Eliud begat Eleazar; and Eleazar begat Matthan; and Matthan begat Jacob;

16 And Jacob begat Joseph the husband of Mary, of whom was born Jesus, who is called Christ.

17 So all the generations from Abraham to David *are* fourteen generations; and from David until the carrying away into Babylon *are* fourteen generations; and from the carrying away into Babylon unto Christ *are* fourteen generations.

—MATTHEW 1:1–17

Above: This detail from a fresco by Giotto depicts the meeting at the Golden Gate of Joachim and Anna, who became the parents of the Virgin Mary.

Jesus' Line of Descent

23 And Jesus himself began to be about thirty years of age, being (as was supposed) the son of Joseph, which was *the son* of Heli,

24 Which was *the son* of Matthat, which was *the son* of Levi, which was *the son* of Melchi, which was *the son* of Janna, which was *the son* of Joseph,

25 Which was *the son* of Mattathias, which was *the son* of Amos, which was *the son* of Naum, which was *the son* of Esli, which was *the son* of Nagge,

26 Which was *the son* of Maath, which was *the son* of Mattathias, which was *the son* of Semei, which was *the son* of Joseph, which was *the son* of Juda,

27 Which was *the son* of Joanna, which was *the son* of Rhesa, which was *the son* of Zorobabel, which was *the son* of Salathiel, which was *the son* of Neri,

28 Which was *the son* of Melchi, which was *the son* of Addi, which was *the son* of Cosam, which was *the son* of Elmodam, which was *the son* of Er,

29 Which was *the son* of Jose, which was *the son* of Eliezer, which was *the son* of Jorim, which was *the son* of Matthat, which was *the son* of Levi,

Right: *An angel prevents Abraham from sacrificing his son, Isaac, in a dramatic scene from the brush of Caravaggio. According to Luke, both of these Jewish patriarchs were ancestors of Jesus.*

30 Which was *the son* of Simeon, which was *the son* of Juda, which was *the son* of Joseph, which was *the son* of Jonan, which was *the son* of Eliakim,

31 Which was *the son* of Melea, which was *the son* of Menan, which was *the son* of Mattatha, which was *the son* of Nathan, which was *the son* of David,

32 Which was *the son* of Jesse, which was *the son* of Obed, which was *the son* of Booz, which was *the son* of Salmon, which was *the son* of Naasson,

33 Which was *the son* of Aminadab, which was *the son* of Aram, which was *the son* of Esrom, which was *the son* of Phares, which was *the son* of Juda,

34 Which was *the son* of Jacob, which was *the son* of Isaac, which was *the son* of Abraham, which was *the son* of Thara, which was *the son* of Nachor,

35 Which was *the son* of Saruch, which was *the son* of Ragau, which was *the son* of Phalec, which was *the son* of Heber, which was *the son* of Sala,

36 Which was *the son* of Cainan, which was *the son* of Arphaxad, which was *the son* of Sem, which was *the son* of Noe, which was *the son* of Lamech,

37 Which was *the son* of Mathusala, which was *the son* of Enoch, which was *the son* of Jared, which was *the son* of Maleleel, which was *the son* of Cainan,

38 Which was *the son* of Enos, which was *the son* of Seth, which was *the son* of Adam, which was *the son* of God.

Above: *Titian's* David and Goliath *(1541). Both Matthew and Luke state that Jesus was descended from David, who was a giant-killing shepherd boy from Bethlehem before becoming king of Israel.*

—LUKE 3:23–38

JOSEPH'S DREAM

18 Now the birth of Jesus Christ was on this wise: When as his mother Mary was espoused to Joseph, before they came together, she was found with child of the Holy Ghost.

19 Then Joseph her husband, being a just *man* and not willing to make her a publick example, was minded to put her away privily.

20 But while he thought on these things, behold, the angel of the Lord appeared unto him in a dream, saying, Joseph, thou son of David, fear not to take unto thee Mary thy wife: for that which is conceived in her is of the Holy Ghost.

21 And she shall bring forth a son, and thou shalt call his name JESUS: for he shall save his people from their sins.

22 Now all this was done, that it might be fulfilled which was spoken of the Lord by the prophet, saying,

23 Behold, a virgin shall be with child, and shall bring forth a son, and they shall call his name Emmanuel, which being interpreted is, God with us.

24 Then Joseph being raised from sleep did as the angel of the Lord had bidden him, and took unto him his wife:

25 And knew her not till she had brought forth her firstborn son: and he called his name JESUS.

—MATTHEW 1:18–25

THE BIRTH OF
IOHN THE BAPTIST

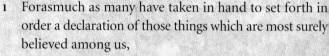

JOHN'S CONCEPTION

1 Forasmuch as many have taken in hand to set forth in order a declaration of those things which are most surely believed among us,

2 Even as they delivered them unto us, which from the beginning were eyewitnesses, and ministers of the word;

3 It seemed good to me also, having had perfect understanding of all things from the very first, to write unto thee in order, most excellent Theophilus,

4 That thou mightest know the certainty of those things, wherein thou hast been instructed.

5 THERE was in the days of Herod, the king of Judaea, a certain priest named Zacharias, of the course of Abia: and his wife *was* of the daughters of Aaron, and her name *was* Elisabeth.

6 And they were both righteous before God, walking in all the commandments and ordinances of the Lord blameless.

7 And they had no child, because that Elisabeth was barren, and they both were *now* well stricken in years.

8 And it came to pass, that while he executed the priest's office before God in the order of his course,

9 According to the custom of the priest's office, his lot was to burn incense when he went into the temple of the Lord.

10 And the whole multitude of the people were praying without at the time of incense.

11 And there appeared unto him an angel of the Lord standing on the right side of the altar of incense.

12 And when Zacharias saw *him*, he was troubled, and fear fell upon him

13 But the angel said unto him, Fear not,

Zacharias: for thy prayer is heard; and thy wife Elisabeth shall bear thee a son, and thou shalt call his name John.

14 And thou shalt have joy and gladness; and many shall rejoice at his birth.

15 For he shall be great in the sight of the Lord, and shall drink neither wine nor strong drink; and he shall be filled with the Holy Ghost, even from his mother's womb.

16 And many of the children of Israel shall he turn to the Lord their God.

17 And he shall go before him in the spirit and power of Elias, to turn the hearts of the fathers to the children, and the disobedient to the wisdom of the just; to make ready a people prepared for the Lord.

18 And Zacharias said unto the angel, Whereby shall I know this? for I am an old man, and my wife well stricken in years.

19 And the angel answering said unto him, I am Gabriel, that stand in the presence of God; and am sent to speak unto thee, and to shew thee these glad tidings.

20 And, behold, thou shalt be dumb, and not able to speak, until the day that these things shall be performed, because thou believest not my words, which shall be fulfilled in their season.

21 And the people waited for Zacharias, and marvelled that he tarried so long in the temple.

22 And when he came out, he could not speak unto them: and they perceived that he had seen a vision in the temple: for he beckoned unto them, and remained speechless.

23 And it came to pass, that, as soon as the days of his ministration were accomplished, he departed to his own house.

24 And after those days his wife Elisabeth conceived, and hid herself five months, saying,

25 Thus hath the Lord dealt with me in the days wherein he looked on me, to take away my reproach among men.

Overleaf: Fra Angelico's charming depiction of the moment when mothers-to-be Mary and Elisabeth (by then six months' pregnant) saluted one another following the Annunciation, as related by Luke (1:39–41).

—LUKE 1:1–25

JOHN'S BIRTH

Opposite: *Perugino's portrayal of the Virgin Mary shows her holding her divine son and enthroned as the queen of heaven. The Madonna and Child are flanked by John the Baptist (on the left) and St. Sebastian (on the right).*

Pages 40–41: *Leonardo da Vinci used artistic license when he depicted the angel appearing to Zacharias amid a throng of people—even if they appear oblivious of the presence of God's messenger in their midst—for Luke says that "the whole multitude of the people were praying without [outside]" (1:10).*

57 Now Elisabeth's full time came that she should be delivered; and she brought forth a son.

58 And her neighbours and her cousins heard how the Lord had shewed great mercy upon her; and they rejoiced with her.

59 And it came to pass, that on the eighth day they came to circumcise the child; and they called him Zacharias, after the name of his father.

60 And his mother answered and said, Not *so*; but he shall be called John.

61 And they said unto her, There is none of thy kindred that is called by this name.

62 And they made signs to his father, how he would have him called.

63 And he asked for a writing table, and wrote, saying, His name is John. And they marvelled all.

64 And his mouth was opened immediately, and his tongue *loosed*, and he spake, and praised God.

65 And fear came on all that dwelt round about them: and all these sayings were noised abroad throughout all the hill country of Judaea.

66 And all they that heard *them* laid *them* up in their hearts, saying, What manner of child shall this be! And the hand of the Lord was with him.

67 And his father Zacharias was filled with the Holy Ghost, and prophesied, saying,

68 Blessed *be* the Lord God of Israel; for he hath visited and redeemed his people,

69 And hath raised up an horn of salvation for us in the house of his servant David;

70 As he spake by the mouth of his holy prophets, which have been since the world began:

71 That we should be saved from our enemies, and from the hand of all that hate us;

72 To perform the mercy *promised* to our fathers, and to

remember his holy covenant;

73 The oath which he sware to our father Abraham,

74 That he would grant unto us, that we being delivered out of the hand of our enemies might serve him without fear,

75 In holiness and righteousness before him, all the days of our life.

76 And thou, child, shalt be called the prophet of the Highest: for thou shalt go before the face of the Lord to prepare his ways;

Page 42: John the Baptist, by Fra Angelico. The script on his banner reads ECCE AGNUS DEI, *the Latin for "Behold, the Lamb of God," the words with which he greeted Jesus.*

77 To give knowledge of salvation unto his people by the remission of their sins,

78 Through the tender mercy of our God; whereby the dayspring from on high hath visited us,

79 To give light to them that sit in darkness and *in* the shadow of death, to guide our feet into the way of peace.

80 And the child grew, and waxed strong in spirit, and was in the deserts till the day of his shewing unto Israel.

—LUKE 1:57–80

The
Annunciation

Previous page:
According to Luke, Mary meekly accepted Gabriel's revelation of God's astonishing plans for her, saying, "Behold the handmaid of the Lord; be it unto me according to thy word" (Luke 1:38).

Right: *The angel Gabriel acts as God's messenger in both the Old and New Testament, and can therefore be seen as a bridge between Heaven and earth, the divine and humankind.*

The Angel Gabriel's Message

26 And in the sixth month the angel Gabriel was sent from God unto a city of Galilee, named Nazareth,

27 To a virgin espoused to a man whose name was Joseph, of the house of David; and the virgin's name *was* Mary.

28 And the angel came in unto her, and said, Hail, *thou that art* highly favoured, the Lord *is* with thee: blessed *art* thou among women.

29 And when she saw *him,* she was troubled at his saying, and cast in her mind what manner of salutation this should be.

30 And the angel said unto her, Fear not, Mary: for thou hast found favour with God.

31 And, behold, thou shalt conceive in thy womb, and bring forth a son, and shalt call his name JESUS.

32 He shall be great, and shall be called the Son of the Highest: and the Lord God shall give unto him the throne of his father David:

33 And he shall reign over the house of Jacob for ever; and of his kingdom there shall be no end.

34 Then said Mary unto the angel, How shall this be, seeing I know not a man?

35 And the angel answered and said unto her, The Holy Ghost shall come upon thee, and the power of the Highest shall overshadow thee: therefore also that holy thing which shall be born of thee shall be called the Son of God.

36 And, behold, thy cousin Elisabeth, she hath also conceived a son in her old age: and this is the sixth month with her, who was called barren.

Left: *Many depictions of the Annunciation, including this one by Titian, show the angel Gabriel holding a white lily, a symbol of the Virgin Mary's purity.*

37 For with God nothing shall be impossible.

38 And Mary said, Behold the handmaid of the Lord; be it unto me according to thy word. And the angel departed from her.

39 And Mary arose in those days, and went into the hill country with haste, into a city of Juda;

40 And entered into the house of Zacharias, and saluted Elisabeth.

41 And it came to pass, that, when Elisabeth heard the salutation of Mary, the babe leaped in her womb; and Elisabeth was filled with the Holy Ghost:

42 And she spake out with a loud voice, and said, Blessed *art* thou among women, and blessed *is* the fruit of thy womb.

43 And whence *is* this to me, that the mother of my Lord should come to me?

44 For, lo, as soon as the voice of thy salutation sounded in mine ears, the babe leaped in my womb for joy.

45 And blessed *is* she that believed: for there shall be a performance of those things which were told her from the Lord.

46 And Mary said, My soul doth magnify the Lord,

47 And my spirit hath rejoiced in God my Saviour.

Below: *Leonardo da Vinci vividly evokes the angel Gabriel's salutation of the Virgin Mary: "Hail, thou that art highly favoured, the Lord is with thee: blessed art thou among women" (Luke 1:28).*

Left: *Fra Angelico's sensitive rendering of the Annunciation. Having informed Mary that she would "bring forth a son" (Luke 1:31), Gabriel went on to tell her that Elisabeth, her elderly cousin "who was called barren" (Luke 1:36), was also expecting a son.*

Below: *During the Annunciation, as depicted below by Caravaggio, the angel Gabriel not only revealed her impending motherhood to the Virgin Mary, but also declared that "that holy thing which shall be born of thee shall be called the Son of God" (Luke 1:35).*

48 For he hath regarded the low estate of his handmaiden: for, behold, from henceforth all generations shall call me blessed.

49 For he that is mighty hath done to me great things; and holy *is* his name.

50 And his mercy *is* on them that fear him from generation to generation.

51 He hath shewed strength with his arm; he hath scattered the proud in the imagination of their hearts.

52 He hath put down the mighty from *their* seats, and exalted them of low degree.

53 He hath filled the hungry with good things; and the rich he hath sent empty away.

54 He hath holpen his servant Israel, in remembrance of *his* mercy;

55 As he spake to our fathers, to Abraham, and to his seed for ever.

56 And Mary abode with her about three months, and returned to her own house.

—LUKE 1:26–56

THE NATIVITY

THE SHEPHERDS

**Previous page,
opposite, and below:**
*Luke's description
of the shepherds'
adoration of the
swaddled Christ
child as he lay in a
manger (Luke 2:16)
has inspired countless
artists, including such
masters as Caravaggio
(previous page) and
Hieronymus Bosch
(opposite), as well
as numerous
children's-book
illustrators (below).*

1 And it came to pass in those days, that there went out a decree from Caesar Augustus, that all the world should be taxed.

2 (*And* this taxing was first made when Cyrenius was governor of Syria.)

3 And all went to be taxed, every one into his own city.

4 And Joseph also went up from Galilee, out of the city of Nazareth, into Judaea, unto the city of David, which is called Bethlehem; (because he was of the house and lineage of David:)

5 To be taxed with Mary his espoused wife, being great with child.

6 And so it was, that, while they were there, the days were accomplished that she should be delivered.

7 And she brought forth her firstborn son, and wrapped him in swaddling clothes, and laid him in a manger; because there was no room for them in the inn.

8 And there were in the same country shepherds abiding in the field, keeping watch over their flock by night.

9 And, lo, the angel of the Lord came upon them, and the glory of the Lord shone round about them: and they were sore afraid.

10 And the angel said unto them, Fear not: for, behold, I bring you good tidings of great joy, which shall be to all people.

11 For unto you is born this day in the city of David a Saviour, which is Christ the Lord.

12 And this *shall* be a sign unto you: Ye shall find the babe wrapped in swaddling clothes, lying in a manger

Right: *Luke tells us that the shepherds hurried to see the "Saviour, which is Christ our Lord" that the angel announced had just been born in the "city of David" (Luke 2:11). By depicting a shepherd holding a lamb, artist Lorenzo di Credi was emphasizing that the Christ child was the "Lamb of God" (John 1:29).*

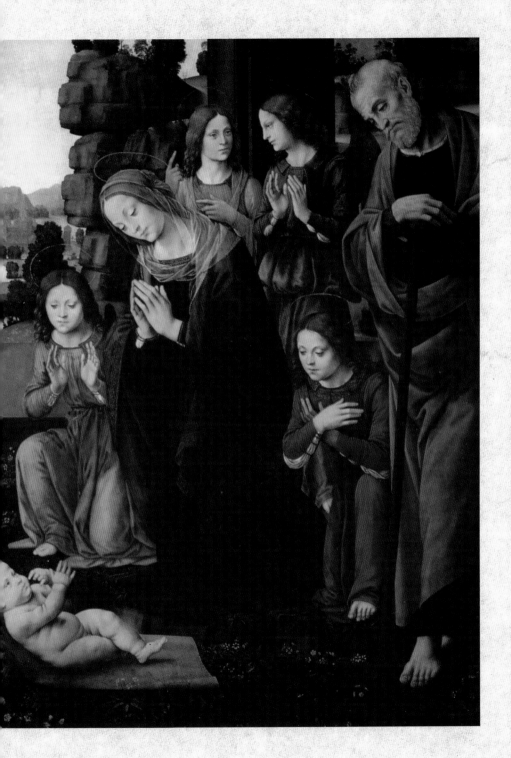

WHILE SHEPHERDS WATCHED

WHILE shepherds watch'd their flocks by night,
All seated on the ground,
The Angel of the LORD came down,
And glory shone around.

"Fear not," said he; for mighty dread
Had seized their troubled mind;
"Glad tidings of great joy I bring
To you and all mankind.

"To you in David's town this day
Is born of David's line
A Saviour, Who is CHRIST the LORD
And this shall be the sign:

"The heav'nly Babe you there shall find
To human view display'd,
All meanly wrapp'd in swathing bands,
And in a manger laid."

Thus spake the seraph; and forthwith
Appear'd a shining throng
Of Angels praising god, who thus
Address'd their joyful song:

"All glory be to GOD on high,
And to the earth be peace:
Good will henceforth from Heav'n to men
Begin and never cease."

13 And suddenly there was with the angel a multitude of the heavenly host praising God, and saying,

14 Glory to God in the highest, and on earth peace, good will toward men.

15 And it came to pass, as the angels were gone away from them into heaven, the shepherds said one to another, Let us now go even unto Bethlehem, and see this thing which is come to pass, which the Lord hath made known unto us.

16 And they came with haste, and found Mary, and Joseph, and the babe lying in a manger.

17 And when they had seen *it*, they made known abroad the saying which was told them concerning this child.

18 And all they that heard *it* wondered at those things which were told them by the shepherds.

19 But Mary kept all these things, and pondered *them* in her heart.

20 And the shepherds returned, glorifying and praising God for all the things that they had heard and seen, as it was told unto them.

—LUKE 2:1–20

Below: *Matthew relates that the star that led the wise men to the baby Jesus "went before them, till it came and stood over where the young child was." (Matthew 2:9).*

THE WISE MEN

*Opposite and below:
All that Matthew tells
us about the Magi is
that they were "wise
men from the east."
Artists have depicted
them in a wide variety
of guises, from old
men to powerful,
wealthy kings.*

1 Now when Jesus was born in Bethlehem of Judaea in the days of Herod the king, behold, there came wise men from the east to Jerusalem,

2 Saying, Where is he that is born King of the Jews? for we have seen his star in the east, and are come to worship him.

3 When Herod the king had heard *these things*, he was troubled, and all Jerusalem with him.

4 And when he had gathered all the chief priests and scribes of the people together, he demanded of them where Christ should be born.

5 And they said unto him, *in* Bethlehem of Judaea: for thus it is written by the prophet,

6 And thou Bethlehem, in the land of Juda, art not the least among the princes of Juda: for out of thee shall come a Governor, that shall rule my people Israel.

7 Then Herod, when he had privily called the wise men, enquired of them diligently what time the star appeared.

8 And he sent them to Bethlehem, and said, Go and search diligently for the young child; and when ye have found *him,* bring me word again, that I may come and worship him also.

9 When they had heard the king, they departed; and, lo, the star, which they saw in the east, went before them, till it came and stood over where the young child was.

10 When they saw the star, they rejoiced with exceeding great joy.

11 And when they were come into the house, they saw the young child with Mary his mother, and fell down, and worshipped him: and when they had opened their treasures, they presented unto him gifts; gold, and frankincense, and myrrh.

12 And being warned of God in a dream that they should not return to Herod, they departed into their own country another way.

—MATTHEW 2:1–12

Opposite: *One of the Magi kneels before the infant Christ in this fifteenth-century painting by Gentile da Fabriano.*

Below: *Velazquez chose to follow a medieval convention, namely depicting one of the wise men as an African king.*

Left: *According to Matthew, when the wise men "saw the young child with Mary his mother," they "fell down and worshipped him: and when they had opened their treasures, they presented unto him gifts; gold, and frankincense, and myrrh" (Matthew 2:11), a scene exquisitely rendered by Botticelli.*

We Three Kings

We three Kings of Orient are:
Bearing gifts we traverse afar
Field and fountain, moor and mountain,
Following yonder star.
O star of wonder, star of night,
Star with royal beauty bright,
Westward leading, still proceeding,
Guide us to Thy perfect light.

Melchior:
Born a King on Bethlehem's plain,
Gold I bring to crown Him again,
King forever, ceasing never,
Over us all to reign.

Caspar:
Frankincense to offer have I,
Incense owns a Deity nigh,
Prayer and praising, all men raising,
Worship Him, God most High.

Balthazar:
Myrrh is mine, its bitter perfume
Breathes a life of gathering gloom:
Sorrowing, sighing, bleeding, dying,
Sealed in the stone-cold tomb.

Glorious now behold Him arise,
King and God and sacrifice,
Alleluia, alleluia;
Earth to the heavens replies.

PRESENTED
AT THE TEMPLE

Simeon and Anna

**Previous page and opposite:** These images of the enthroned Madonna and Child are by the Italian artist Giovanni da Fiesole (c.1387–1455). Better known today as Fra Angelico ("the Angelic Brother"), da Fiesole was a Dominican friar whose piety is evident in his work.

21 And when eight days were accomplished for the circumcising of the child, his name was called JESUS, which was so named of the angel before he was conceived in the womb.

22 And when the days of her purification according to the law of Moses were accomplished, they brought _him_ to Jerusalem, to present him to the Lord;

23 (As it is written in the law of the Lord, Every male that openeth the womb shall be called holy to the Lord;)

24 And to offer a sacrifice according to that which is said in the law of the Lord, A pair of turtledoves, or two young pigeons.

25 And, behold, there was a man in Jerusalem, whose name was Simeon; and the same man _was_ just and devout, waiting for the consolation of Israel: and the Holy Ghost was upon him.

26 And it was revealed unto him by the Holy Ghost, that he should not see death, before he had seen the Lord's Christ.

27 And he came by the Spirit into the temple: and when the parents brought in the child Jesus, to do for him after the custom of the law,

28 Then took he him up in his arms, and blessed God, and said,

29 Lord, now lettest thou thy servant depart in peace, according to thy word:

30 For mine eyes have seen thy salvation,

31 Which thou hast prepared before the face of all people;

32 A light to lighten the Gentiles, and the glory of thy people Israel.

33 And Joseph and his mother marvelled at those things which were spoken of him.

34 And Simeon blessed them, and said unto Mary his mother, Behold, this _child_ is set for the fall and rising again of many in Israel; and for a sign which shall be spoken against;

35 (Yea, a sword shall pierce through thy own soul also,) that the thoughts of many hearts may be revealed.

36 And there was one Anna, a prophetess, the daughter of Phanuel, of the tribe of Aser: she was of a great age, and had lived with an husband seven years from her virginity.

37 And she *was* a widow of about fourscore and four years,

Right: *Luke tells us that when Joseph and Mary (far left) brought Jesus to the temple "to present him to the Lord" (Luke 2:22), both Simeon and Anna (far right) hailed the infant as the Messiah.*

which departed not from the temple, but served *God* with fastings and prayers night and day.

38 And she coming in that instant gave thanks likewise unto the Lord, and spake of him to all them that looked for redemption in Jerusalem.

—LUKE 2:21–38

Below: Giotto's Madonna is holding a white rose, a symbol of her virginity, or purity, as well as of her status as the "rose of heaven" of Christian tradition.

ESCAPING
TO SAFETY

THE FLIGHT INTO EGYPT

Previous page:
Joseph prioritized the safety of his wife and her child. Indeed, had it not been for Joseph, Jesus might have perished during Herod's Massacre of the Innocents.

Right: *Fra Angelico's vision of the Holy Family's Flight into Egypt, with Mary and Jesus riding to safety on a donkey and Joseph trudging along behind them.*

13 And when they [the wise men, or magi] were departed, behold, the angel of the Lord appeareth to Joseph in a dream, saying, Arise, and take the young child and his mother, and flee into Egypt, and be thou there until I bring thee word: for Herod will seek the young child to destroy him.

14 When he arose, he took the young child and his mother by night, and departed into Egypt:

15 And was there until the death of Herod: that it might be fulfilled which was spoken of the Lord by the prophet, saying, Out of Egypt have I called my son.

16 Then Herod, when he saw that he was mocked of the wise men, was exceeding wroth, and sent forth, and slew all the children that were in Bethlehem, and in all the coasts thereof, from two years old and

Right: Matthew says that the Holy Family fled to Egypt "that it might be fulfilled which was spoken of the Lord by the prophet, saying, Out of Egypt have I called my son" (Matthew 2:15). The prophet to whom Matthew is referring is Hosea (see Hosea 11:1).

The Glory of the Nativity

Opposite: *Raphael's portrayal of the Madonna and Child.*

Below: *Caravaggio's interpretation of the rest stop that the Holy Family were said to have taken on the way.*

under, according to the time which he had diligently inquired of the wise men.

17 Then was fulfilled that which was spoken by Jeremy the prophet, saying,

18 In Rama was there a voice heard, lamentation, and weeping, and great mourning, Rachel weeping *for* her children, and would not be comforted, because they are not.

—MATTHEW 2:13–18

THE RETURN OF THE HOLY FAMILY TO NAZARETH

19 But when Herod was dead, behold, an angel of the Lord appeareth in a dream to Joseph in Egypt,

20 Saying, Arise, and take the young child and his mother, and go into the land of Israel: for they are dead which sought the young child's life.

21 And he arose, and took the young child and his mother, and came into the land of Israel.

22 But when he heard that Archelaus did reign in Judaea in the room of his father Herod, he was afraid to go thither: notwithstanding, being warned of God in a dream, he turned aside into the parts of Galilee:

23 And he came and dwelt in a city called Nazareth: that it might be fulfilled which was spoken by the prophets, He shall be called a Nazarene.

—MATTHEW 2:19–23

39 And when they had performed all things according to the law of the Lord, they returned into Galilee, to their own city Nazareth.

40 And the child grew, and waxed strong in spirit, filled with wisdom: and the grace of God was upon him.

—LUKE 2:39–40

Opposite: *"And Mary said, My soul doth magnify the Lord, And my spirit hath rejoiced in God my Saviour. For he hath regarded the low estate of his handmaiden: for, behold, from henceforth all generations shall call me blessed"* *(Luke 1:46–48).*

INDEX